W9-CKU-464

JAWSOME
SHARK
QUIZZES

JAWSOME SHARK QUIZZES

Test Your Knowledge of Shark Types, Behaviors, Attacks, Myths and Other Trivia

Karen Chu

Ulysses Press

Text copyright © 2017 Karen Chu. Design and concept copyright © 2017 Ulysses Press and its licensors. All rights reserved. Any unauthorized duplication in whole or in part or dissemination of this edition by any means (including but not limited to photocopying, electronic devices, digital versions, and the Internet) will be prosecuted to the fullest extent of the law.

Published in the United States by
ULYSSES PRESS
P.O. Box 3440
Berkeley, CA 94703
www.ulyssespress.com

ISBN: 978-1-61243-684-5
Library of Congress Control Number 2016957495

Printed in the United States by United Graphics, Inc.
10 9 8 7 6 5 4 3 2 1

Acquisitions Editor: Casie Vogel
Managing Editor: Claire Chun
Project Editor: Alice Riegert
Editor: Renee Rutledge
Proofreader: Shayna Keyles
Cover and interior layout and design: what!design @ whatweb.com
Cover artwork: shark's teeth © daulon/shutterstock.com; shark feeding
    frenzy © melissaf84/shutterstock.com
Interior artwork: see page 245

Distributed by Publishers Group West

This book is independently authored and published. No endorsement or sponsorship by or affiliation with movies, celebrities, products, or other copyright and trademark holders is claimed or suggested. All references in this book to copyrighted or trademarked characters and other elements of movies and products are for the purpose of commentary, criticism, analysis, and literary discussion only.

TABLE OF CONTENTS

TIME TO DROP YOUR JAW TO JAWS

Sharks have captivated our hearts, our imaginations, and sometimes, our nightmares: their beady eyes, their brute power in the water, and of course, let's not forget their maws full of spiky, serrated terror. Sharks seem mythological and unreal, like something we made up in our heads. *Hey! Imagine a fish that doesn't have any bones; some can glow in the dark, some can live over 100 years, some have 300 teeth, some weigh as much as ten cars!*

But the unbelievable thing is, they do exist! The truth is oftentimes stranger than fiction. But what we think we know about sharks is just the tip of the dorsal fin. The world of mind-blowing shark facts is as expansive as the waters they live in. Ready for your dive? Then open those brain gates up to let the shark facts flood in, and test your shark fintelligence.

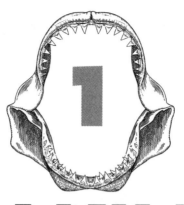

1

MAKING WAVES IN SCHOOL

SPECIES AND GENERAL SHARK TRIVIA

PICK YOUR PREY

Calling all shark aficionados (or maybe a-fish-ionados)! Let's dive in and test your smarts in this multiple-choice quiz that's all about the basics: general shark facts and the diverse world of shark species.

1. *One fish, two fish, blue fish, red fish.* Just how many different species of sharks are there in existence?

A. 5

B. 50

C. 500

ANSWER: C. 500

Ah-may-zing. There are around 500 different species of sharks, and they come in all sorts of shapes, sizes, and colors, from the iconic, fearsome great white to the docile, gentle zebra shark, from the portable, palm-sized pygmy shark to the bubblegum-pink deepwater goblin shark. What most people picture when they think "shark" is only a small fraction of all the incredible species out there!

2. Time to get (meta)physical: When do sharks become *sharks*? The term "shark" in taxonomy refers to all the shark species within the same level of various:

A. Classes

B. Orders

C. Families

ANSWER: B. Orders

Kingdom > Phylum > Class > Order > Family > Genus > Species. The animal we call "shark" starts getting defined right after the class *Chondrichthyes* (which describes all cartilaginous fish). So the term "shark" refers to all members within eight different orders under the collective superorder name of *Selachimorpha*.

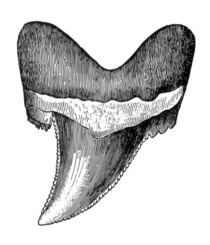

3. Quick, tell me: Scientifically, are rays classified as sharks?

YES! Not many people know that they are also part of this cartilaginous fish family.

NOPE. The way the rays and sharks breathe are different.

ANSWER: B. Nope

There are three main types of fish that have skeletons made of cartilage instead of bone: sharks, rays, and chimaeras. Even though sharks and rays share the same class (*Chondrichthyes*), one of the main differences that sets the two apart is the location of their gills. Since rays are flat and are bottom-feeders, they draw in water from openings on top of their heads to their gills located at the bottom, whereas sharks have gills on the sides (or in the case of the angel shark, on the top) of their bodies.

4. True or false: Sharks are loners and never live in groups.

TRUE. Other than mating and feeding, sharks operate on their own.

FALSE. Like birds and insects, some shark species migrate together annually.

ANSWER: B. False

Though it is true that there really isn't a permanent social structure in place for sharks, there are instances when sharks do travel or work together. Some shark species might pair up to hunt together. Young hammerheads stick together until they're older and bigger. There are some sharks that migrate together to warmer waters during their mating seasons, like the blacktip sharks who show up in the thousands and pepper the Florida coast every winter.

5. A parliament of owls, a gaggle of geese, an unkindness of ravens...and a group of sharks is called a:

A. Risk

B. Murder

C. Shiver

ANSWER: C. Shiver

A group of sharks can also be generically referred to as a gam, school, or herd. But the other two options are real collective nouns too: a *risk* of lobsters and a *murder* of crows.

6. True or false: The great white shark has no known natural predators.

TRUE

FALSE

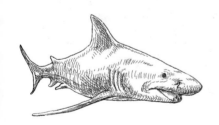

ANSWER: B. False

It's actually a very common misconception that great white sharks have no predators! Killer whales, or orcas, have been spotted a few times successfully killing and feasting on great white sharks. Reports of declining great white shark populations often occur where orca pods hang out. The killer whale definitely is a true apex predator (and the name sure makes a lot of sense now).

7. How much more likely are you to be struck by lightning than eaten by a shark?

A. 3 times more

B. 13 times more

C. 30 times more

ANSWER: C. 30 times more

Hard to believe that in the US, there was only one human death (in Hawaii) from a shark attack in 2015 while almost 30 people died nationally from being struck by lightning. It's important to note that sharks rarely attack humans for food. Sharks are curious when they encounter something unusual on their turf, and the only way they can explore an object or organism is to bite it, whether it's a boat, a person, or an abandoned car tire. Rarely do they seek out humans for feeding.

8. And speaking of the grim matter, which country ranks the highest in documented fatal shark attacks?

A. Brazil

B. United States

C. Australia

ANSWER: C. Australia

Here's a good Poindexter tidbit to impress fellow shark fans: Though Australia ranks the highest in death count, the United States holds the record for most documented nonfatal shark attacks. Florida and California are two of the most shark-infested regions in the world.

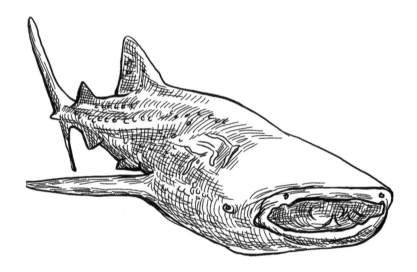

9. A swellshark is a species of shark named after what unique feature?

A. It sucks in water to enlarge its belly twice its size when threatened.

B. It can give birth to up to 90 shark babies and looks very swollen when pregnant.

C. It can fill its body with extra air to quickly float up to the surface for food.

ANSWER: A. It sucks in water.

When filled with water, the swellshark takes on a snowman-like shape...well, snowman with a tail. And swellsharks are actually oviparous; they lay eggs instead of giving birth to live young. Their eggs are enclosed in a bizarrely shaped leathery case with hooks and tendrils that's commonly known as a "mermaid's purse."

10. Though there are hundreds of non-aggressive types of sharks, there are four main shark species that are considered the most aggressive and have collectively caused almost all recorded unprovoked attacks: the great white, the bull shark, the tiger shark, and what lesser-known shark that Jacques Cousteau described as "the most dangerous of all sharks"?

A. Oceanic whitetip

B. Blue shark

C. Caribbean reef shark

ANSWER: A. Oceanic whitetip

Even though the oceanic whitetip is aggressive, there haven't been that many documented whitetip attacks. That's because shark experts suspect that oceanic whitetips are mostly responsible for attacking survivors of shipwrecks out at sea, and those fatal incidents go unrecorded. There were cases like *RMS Nova Scotia* and the *USS Indianapolis* during World War II where sailors managed to survive the ship's attack but unfortunately fell victim to predating oceanic whitetip sharks amidst the wreckage.

11. *Isistius brasiliensis* is a unique smaller shark species that gets food by latching onto prey and gouging out round, circular chunks of flesh. It's commonly known as the:

A. Cookiecutter shark

B. Hole-puncher shark

C. Driller shark

ANSWER: A. Cookiecutter shark

Reminiscent of the creepy, beady-eyed *Alien* chest burster, the tube-like cookiecutter shark will pretty much try to twist its circular open jaw around anything: seals, whales, other larger sharks, fish nets, and yes, even submarines...which is one of the main reasons why submarines are now coated in fiberglass.

12. Though the river shark is the only true freshwater shark, what famously aggressive type of shark can survive in both salt water and freshwater, and can basically hang out in rivers?

A. Great white

B. Bull shark

C. Tiger shark

ANSWER: B. Bull shark

Bull sharks are *diadromous*, meaning they can easily switch back and forth from salt water and freshwater environments. They achieve this by expelling 20 times more urine when in freshwater to maintain the salt balance in their bodies. It's quite an impressive pee break.

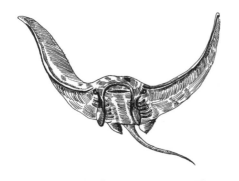

13. Another odd family of sharks is thresher sharks, named for that gigantic scythe-shaped tail that takes up half of the whole shark length. Obviously, the thresher shark is not going to put on a little farmer hat and reap farm crops with its huge tail; what, then, is it used for?

A. To forcefully whip prey into a stunned state

B. To slice off kelp and other seaweed for food

C. To fool predators into thinking that the shark is a lot bigger than it really is

ANSWER: A. To whip

It's quite an amazing sight when the thresher shark decides to strike. Sneaking swiftly into a giant school of fish, the shark can whip its tail so hard it can knock out dozens of fish for a tasty feast.

14. As of 2016, there were around 70 species of sharks officially listed as vulnerable to extinction. What has been the biggest threat to sharks?

A. Being hunted for shark fin

B. Overfishing

C. Marine pollution

ANSWER: B. Overfishing

Technically, the biggest threat to sharks is, sadly, humans. All answer options contribute to the declining populations of shark species, and all are caused by humans. Overfishing, though, is perhaps the most serious issue. An estimated 70 million sharks are killed by people every year due to commercial fishing, recreational fishing, and "by-catch," where sharks are unintentionally caught. Sharks have tremendous difficulty recovering their populations after extreme depletions due to their long maturation rate and low birth rate.

15. What type of shark is called *marokintana,* which translates to "many stars" in Malagasy, one of the official languages in Madagascar?

A. Star-spotted smooth-hound

B. Leopard shark

C. Whale shark

ANSWER: C. Whale shark

Several cultures around the world have very evocative and descriptive names for the whale shark due to its brilliant white spots. In Swahili, whale sharks are called *papa shillingi*. The story goes that angels were so happy with whale sharks that they threw shillings, and the coins got stuck on the sharks' backs.

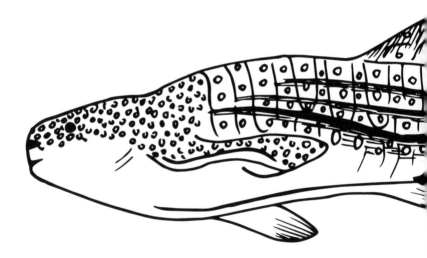

16. Are there really plenty of fish in the sea? Now that you know there are around 500 different species of sharks, how many new species of sharks were discovered just in 2015?

A. 0

B. 6

C. 30

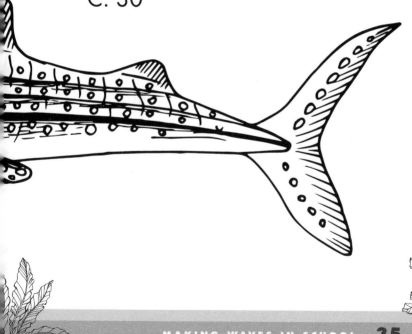

# ANSWER: B. 6

It's crazy to think biologists are still discovering new species of sharks! New species include both sharks that humans have never seen before and existing sharks that have not been studied extensively enough to be properly named or categorized. Team Shark's Class of 2015 includes five various catsharks and one very strange ninja lanternshark (named for its tremendously dark, jet black skin).

17. Great white sharks are amazingly efficient: They are very aware of what kind of prey will provide the nutrients they need and will reject food that doesn't match their nutritional needs (thus saving energy). Which of the following prey animal will a shark most likely reject?

A. Seal

B. Pig

C. Sheep

ANSWER: C. Sheep

Shark expert Peter Klimley actually did conduct a test of providing great whites with bodies of a seal, a pig, and a sheep. Great white sharks opt for prey with high fat content, so their usual diet includes seals, fatty fish, and blubbery whales.

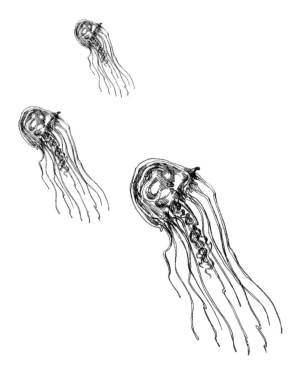

18. What is the most common and most populous shark species in the world?

A. Spiny dogfish

B. Grey reef shark

C. Blacktip reef shark

ANSWER: A. Spiny dogfish

Even though it is the most common type of shark right now, the small spiny dogfish is not as abundant as it used to be and has been suffering a sharp decline in population due to overfishing. It's fished for meat, fins, oil, cartilage, and even for biology dissections in schools.

19. Who's the boss? How do sharks usually determine social rank?

A. By body size

B. By swimming speed

C. By the size of their prey

ANSWER: A. By body size

Normally, sharks ride solo, and even in temporary group settings, they typically don't get into fights for dominance. But in cases of mating and feeding, larger sharks do take the proverbial cake.

20. There's a remote oceanic area between Mexico and Hawaii that serves as a frequent hangout spot for a specific aggressive species of sharks. Experts still have not determined why this place is so popular among these sharks. What nickname did marine biologists give to this happenin' spot?

A. White Shark Café

B. The Bull Pen

C. Tiger Shark Tavern

ANSWER: A. White Shark Café

It's pretty weird! This area has very little food for the white sharks, so researchers find it odd that many of the tagged or tracked white sharks swim all the way there to hang out. Also, this would make for a terrific sitcom: six shark friends talking about their life at a café–let's call the show *Chums*.

21. The *Cretoxyrhina* lived during the Cretaceous Period 100 million years ago and were known for having extremely hard teeth. Uncovered fossils have shown that the *Cretoxyrhina*'s teeth had an unusually thick covering of enamel, which could likely cut through bone and shell as easily as it could through flesh. Given this feature of their teeth, this prehistoric shark earned what knife-related nickname?

A. Ginsu shark

B. Samurai shark

C. Katana shark

ANSWER: A. Ginsu shark

But wait, there's more! These super sharp kitchen knives were sold via late night TV ads and paved the way for modern infomercial pitches. Though having a nickname inspired by an infomercial product may seem silly, the Ginsu shark's ferocity sure isn't. There are records of *Cretoxyrhina* teeth found in the skeletons of mesosaurs. So this particular shark may have been a dinosaur eater!

WELCOME TO THE SHARK OLYMPICS!

Sharks! Sharks! We've got sharks. We've got sharks that glow. We've got sharks that jump. But which notable sharks are record holders in the underwater kingdom? Match the following superlative with the corresponding shark title winner.

Largest living	Blue shark
Largest extinct	Bull shark
Smallest	Dwarf lanternshark
Fastest	Greenland shark
Strongest bite	Megalodon
Deepest diver	Portuguese dogfish
Largest litter	Whale shark
Longest living	Mako shark

ANSWER:

LARGEST LIVING: Whale shark. The largest confirmed individual had a length of 41.5 feet (12.65 meters) and a weight of about 47,000 pounds (about the weight of 10 cars!).

LARGEST EXTINCT: Megalodon. Scientists have been able to estimate the length of this giant extinct shark by studying reconstructed jaw fossils that are truly massive. The common consensus is that megalodons probably measured about 59 feet (18 meters long).

SMALLEST: Dwarf lanternshark. This wee species not only can produce light from photophores on their bodies, but can fit on the palm of your hand! The maximum known length of this shark is only 8 inches (20 centimeters) long.

FASTEST: Mako shark. The shortfin mako shark has a recorded speed of 25 mph (40 km/h) with bursts of speed of almost double.

STRONGEST BITE: Bull shark. Pound per pound, bull sharks have the largest bite force value among studied sharks. Mature bull shark bites can reach up to a maximum force equivalent to almost 1,350 pounds-force, or 6,000 newtons. For comparison, an average human bite is 120 pounds-force, or 534 newtons.

DEEPEST DIVER: Portuguese dogfish. This smaller species of shark is the deepest living shark currently known, sometimes living in depths of 2.3 miles or 3.7 kilometers below the surface! In order to survive the dark ocean depths, the Portuguese dogfish has amazingly strong vision in the dark to detect prey.

LARGEST LITTER: Blue shark. A blue shark once was reported to have a litter of 135 in her uterus. A real *motherload.*

LONGEST LIVING: Greenland shark. Man, they're old! These sharks can live for hundreds of years! Thanks to extensive study, shark biologists have estimated the oldest Greenland shark specimen to be 392 years old (give or take 120 years, due to radiocarbon dating). And the Greenland shark carries the title of longest living vertebrate in the world.

TAKE A SWIM ON THE WILD SIDE

With over 500 different species, a lot of sharks have been weirdly named after other animals due to similar appearance and/or nature. Which of the following three are not real shark names? Circle your three guesses!

DOGFISH

HOUND SHARK

TIGER SHARK

BULL SHARK

SALMON SHARK

WOLFFISH

CROCODILE SHARK

WHALE SHARK

ZEBRA SHARK

COBRA SHARK

WEASEL SHARK

PIGEYE SHARK

DALMATIAN SHARK

CATSHARK

LEOPARD SHARK

FROG SHARK

COW SHARK

ANSWER:

The **WOLFFISH**, **COBRA SHARK**, and **DALMATIAN SHARK** are not sharks, although the real wolffish is an eel-looking bottomfeeder bony fish. Here's more information about the rest of the wild bunch:

DOGFISH. Named for their canine-like behavior and pack aggression during feeding

HOUND SHARK. And speaking of dogs, another shark with a canine name!

TIGER SHARK. Named for the dark stripes that run down their bodies

BULL SHARK. Named for their bulky, extremely wide bodies and unpredictable, aggressive demeanor

SALMON SHARK. Named for its salmon-heavy diet

CROCODILE SHARK. Named for how the shark forcefully snaps when taken out of the water

WHALE SHARK. Named for its similarities to a whale—slow moving, massive, and gentle

ZEBRA SHARK. This shark threw off early taxonomists, since only the young sharks had a zebra-like

pattern of white bands across a dark body. When fully grown, the stripes disappear and result in more of a spotted leopard look.

WEASEL SHARK. Named for its relatively small but long body and snout

PIGEYE SHARK. It's uncertain if this shark is named after its pig-like eyes, but this species is commonly mistaken for the bull shark.

CATSHARK. Named for its feline eyes and nocturnal habits. A special shout-out goes to a shark that's named after both an animal *and* a candy: the lollipop catshark, which refers to its round body and tapered tail.

LEOPARD SHARK. Named for its dark spots and bronze-gray skin color

FROG SHARK. Not much is known about these deep-sea sharks, and there have only been a handful of recorded catches.

COW SHARK. This family of deep-sea sharks is characterized by a bulky body and round snout, and is considered as the most primitive of all the sharks due to similarities with ancient extinct species.

WHEN ANIMALS ATTACK

Though there are extremely fearsome sharks capable of some real hurt, shark attacks are not as common as one would think. Human deaths by sharks are actually quite low when compared to other animal attacks. So what animals are more likely to kill you? Rank the following animal culprits, whose attacks caused the most human deaths in the US, from high to low.

ANIMAL CULPRITS:

COWS & HORSES

CROCODILES & ALLIGATORS

DOGS

HORNETS, WASPS, & BEES

SHARKS

SNAKES & LIZARDS

VENOMOUS SPIDERS

HIGHEST NUMBER OF DEATHS

1. _____

2. _____

3. _____

4. _____

5. _____

6. _____

7. _____

LOWEST NUMBER OF DEATHS

ANSWER:

1. Cows & horses (655 deaths)

2. Hornets, wasps, & bees (509 deaths)

3. Dogs (250 deaths)

4. Snakes & lizards (136 deaths)

5. Venomous spiders (70 deaths)

6. Crocodiles & alligators (9 deaths)

7. Sharks (8 deaths)

There are a couple factors that come into play when studying animal attacks. Though sharks and crocodiles can be frightening, the chance of encountering those animals for an average person is quite low. More deaths occur from popular and more common animals that humans are constantly around, which raises the attack rate statistic. Many of the deaths caused by cows and horses occur (unsurprisingly) on farms and ranches where humans are in constant contact with these animals. And when you're out in the wild, definitely know your allergies and dress accordingly! Most of the fatal animal attacks that happen in the wilderness are caused by reactions from venomous insects, snakes, and spiders.

(Source: Wilderness and Environmental Medicine analysis of CDC statistics, 1999–2007.)

WHAT'S IN A NAME?

Well, turns out a lot is in a shark's common name. Shark experts are pretty matter-of-fact when it comes to nomenclature. For example, the sharpnose sevengill shark is named for, well...its seven pairs of gills and its sharp nose. But with such a tremendous variety of unique shark species, these names can get pretty specific. See if you can guess these real shark names from a description of their appearance and/or behavior. Don't worry, to help you out, we filled in all the letters that are S, H, A, R, and K.

EXAMPLE: These sharks from the family *Sphyrnidae* have eyes located on side protrusions on their noggins, giving them 360-degree vertical vision as well as a hardware-inspired name.

H A <u>M</u> <u>M</u> E R H E <u>A</u> <u>D</u>   S H A R K

1. These *Orectolobiformes* order of sharks are commonly named for their intricate and geometric flat patterns that "really tie the room together." They tend to reside in seabeds and on ocean floors.

_ A R _ _ _   S H A R K

2. Biologist Leonard Compagno named this shark after a throaty J. R. R. Tolkien character, noting some similarities in appearance and behavior.

_ _ _ _ _ _ S H A R K

3. The members of this family all have light-producing organs in their bodies, so these smallish sharks glow in the dark depths of the ocean.

_ A _ _ _ R _   S H A R K

4. In India, it's believed that eating this shark's flesh can enhance lactation.

_ _ _ K   S H A R K

5. This cute little deepwater thing is not named after its portable size, but after the two pouches in front of its fins. No one knows what the pouches are for, but it's definitely not for tiny wallets and keys.

_ _ _ K _ _ SHARK

6. The *Somniosidae* family are characterized by their groggy movement, lazzzzzzzy slow speed, and nonaggressive nature. *Yawn.*

S _ _ _ _ _ R SHARK

7. This catshark features a trippy, diamond-like repeating pattern that's very reminiscent of old clowns and jesters.

_ A R _ _ _ _ _ _ SHARK

8. How luxurious! The skin on this kind of shark feels super smooth and satiny.

S _ _ K _   S H A R K

9. It looks like a giant rubbery sock puppet, and it's the smallest of three plankton-eating shark species in existence (whale shark and basking shark being the other two); it gets its name from its comically large maw that is not at all mini.

_ _ _ A _ _ _ _ H   S H A R K

10. Warning! Warning! This animal is actually not a shark at all—it's technically a chimaera, another type of cartilaginous fish. Their pale eyes and ethereal milky blue skin earned them this eerie name.

_ H _ S _ SHARK

11. Scientists struggled for decades to figure out what part of the *Helicoprion* shark a specific spiny whorl fossil belongs to. (Imagine a spiraling disk covered in serrated, sharp protrusions.) Well, turns out this circular disk of nightmare teeth is lodged in this shark's lower jaw, helping the *Helicoprion* earn this power tool nickname.

_ _ _ _ SA _ SHARK

ANSWER:

1. Carpet
2. Gollum
3. Lantern
4. Milk
5. Pocket
6. Sleeper
7. Harlequin
8. Silky
9. Megamouth
10. Ghost

(It's important/wacky to note that chimaeras don't have teeth, and the males have a retractable penis-like dongle on their head.)

11. Buzzsaw

CRYPTOQUOTE
PART 1

Time to dip your fins into some cryptography and cipher puzzle solving. Here we have a moving quote about sharks, but it's all encrypted! Each letter stands for another. Try to look for certain letter patterns: single letters by themselves are probably an A or and I, contractions usually are -'RE, -'NT, or -'VE, and of course, the word "SHARK" appears a few times. Unused letters are noted as well.

PUZZLE LETTER = ANSWER LETTER

A =   J = not used   S =

B =   K =   T =

C =   L =   U =

D =   M = not used   W =

E =   N =   V = not used

F =   O =   X = not used

G =   P = not used   Y =

H = not used   Q =   Z = not used

I =   R =

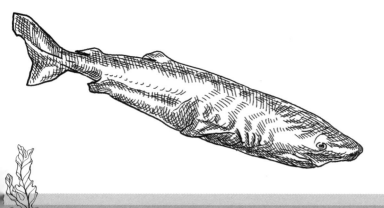

"FGOQCF OQB WBOKEASKI
_ _ _ _ _ _   _ _ _   _ _ _ _ _ _ _ _ _
ORANOIF, ORU AS TLK'QB
_ _ _ _ _ _ _ _ ,   _ _ _   _ _   _ _ _ _ _
IKDCT BRLKYG EL FBB ILEF LS
_ _ _ _ _   _ _ _ _ _ _   _ _   _ _ _   _ _ _ _   _ _
EGBN, EGOE NBORF EGOE
_ _ _ _ ,   _ _ _ _   _ _ _ _ _   _ _ _ _
TLK'QB AR O GBOIEGT LDBOR.
_ _ _ _ _   _ _   _   _ _ _ _ _ _ _   _ _ _ _ _ .
TLK FGLKIU WB OSQOAU AS
_ _ _   _ _ _ _ _ _   _ _   _ _ _ _ _ _   _ _
TLK OQB AR EGB LDBOR ORU
_ _ _   _ _ _   _ _   _ _ _   _ _ _ _ _   _ _ _
ULR'E FBB FGOQCF."
_ _ _ _ ,   _ _ _   _ _ _ _ _ _ . "

—Sylvia Earle, marine biologist,
and *National Geographic*'s Explorer-in-Residence

ANSWER:

A = I

B = E

C = K

D = C

E = T

F = S

G = H

H = not used

I = L

J = not used

K = U

L = O

M = not used

N = M

O = A

P = not used

Q = R

R = N

S = F

T = Y

U = D

W = B

V = not used

X = not used

Y = G

Z = not used

"SHARKS ARE BEAUTIFUL ANIMALS, AND IF YOU'RE LUCKY ENOUGH TO SEE LOTS OF THEM, THAT MEANS THAT YOU'RE IN A HEALTHY OCEAN. YOU SHOULD BE AFRAID IF YOU ARE IN THE OCEAN AND DON'T SEE SHARKS."

—Sylvia Earle, marine biologist,
and *National Geographic*'s Explorer-in-Residence

WHAT A
FINTASTIC
BODY

ANATOMY AND
REPRODUCTION

SINK OR SWIM?

The colorful and bizarre diversity of shark species is characterized by some pretty interesting and unique anatomical features. Put on some John Mayer and discover how the shark body is truly a wonderland. And watch out for trick questions!

1. ● Gotta go fast! Sharks are able to glide through the water with super efficiency, thanks to what odd feature found on their skin?

A. A slick coating of oil that actually smells like old bananas

B. A smooth, rubbery epidermis layer like a dolphin's

C. Millions of tiny teeth on their skin

ANSWER: C. Millions of tiny teeth

Yes, shark skin is covered with "denticles," which might look like scales, but are really a tight array of mini teeth. Denticles help reduce turbulence and boost thrust, allowing the shark to swim not only faster, but also more quietly and sneakily. Even Speedo got the memo and put out a line of wetsuits and swimsuits inspired by the shark's unique toothy skin.

2. They're not fat! They're just....*oily.* Sharks have a lot of oil in their bodies. What is it primarily used for?

A. To help their skin repel water in order to swim faster

B. To keep their bodies buoyant in water

C. To keep their bodies warm in cold temperatures

ANSWER: B. To keep their bodies buoyant

Unlike most fish, sharks do not have a swim bladder, a gas-filled organ that looks like a balloon animal. Swim bladders help fish control their buoyancy, allowing them to float in water at different vertical levels. Instead, shark livers contain a lot of oil to help them control floating, and in some sharks, oil accounts for up to 20 percent of body weight. However, sand tiger sharks employ a makeshift swim bladder by storing air in their stomachs.

3. The most distinct characterization for the entire shark family is that instead of bones, their skeletons are made up of cartilage, a rubbery, solid tissue. What part of your body is also composed of mostly cartilage?

A. Nose

B. Tongue

C. Eyeball

ANSWER: A. Nose

If you touch and push the tip of your nose, you can tell that even though it's firm, it still has a flexible quality to it. The only bone-like part on a shark is its teeth. Since cartilage disintegrates way easier and faster than calcium-laden bones do in salt water, in most of the shark's fossilized remains, only of the jaws and teeth are found.

4. Rays can see color, but aquatic mammals like whales and dolphins can't. So tell me, do most sharks see color?

YES, duh—most fish can see color, even ultraviolet.

NO, sharks are just not that #blessed.

ANSWER: B. No

Recent studies have shown that most sharks cannot distinguish color. Long story short, eyes are mostly made up of rods (photoreceptors that capture low light wavelengths) and cones (photoreceptors that to capture higher light wavelength for color). Most sharks only have a single rod photoreceptor and no cones at all. So really, that's just another similarity between sharks and your color-blind dog.

5. How many different types of fins do most sharks have?

A. Two

B. Five

C. Seven

ANSWER: B. Five

Most sharks have five types of fins: a pair of pectoral fins (flippers), a pair of pelvic fins, two dorsal fins on top, an anal fin, and a caudal fin (tail). Of course, some sharks differ, and the number of fins is often a determinant of what order the species belongs to.

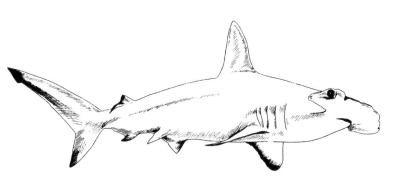

6. The fastest species of shark is the shortfin mako. It has a recorded speed of 25 mph and can thrust itself into bursts of up to 46 mph. What other special ability does the shortfin mako shark have that truly makes it even more terrifying?

A. It can emit a sound similar to a high-pitched scream.

B. It can jump completely out of the water.

C. It can camouflage itself to look invisible under water.

ANSWER: B. It can jump.

The shortfin mako can jump. No, not jump, *leap* as tall as 9 meters out of the water. And it has been reported to be able to jump and land its 200 pound-ish body *onto boats*!

7. Most sharks are poikilothermic, which is a fancier and more technical way of saying that sharks are:

A. Cold-blooded

B. Warm-blooded

C. Hot-blooded

ANSWER: A. Cold-blooded

Warm-bloodedness (chiefly in mammals and birds) refers to having a constant body temperature that's usually higher than that of the surroundings. Cold-bloodedness, however, is a bit of a misnomer because the blood is not always "cold." Generally, cold-blooded animals are described as able to survive in a wider range of temperatures, and their blood temperature is dependent on and varies with their environment. But not all sharks are poikilothermic; some, like the great white and mako, have metabolisms that generate heat internally.

8. Is there such a thing as albino sharks–as in, sharks that have no pigment in their bodies and appear to be white or flesh-colored with pink eyes?

NO, albinism only happens in mammals and some birds.

YES, technically it can happen due to genetics, but they are rarely seen.

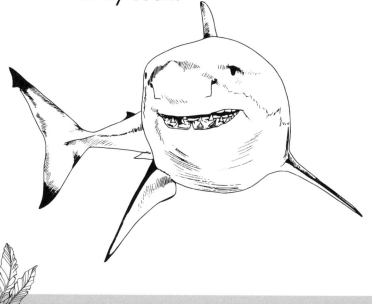

ANSWER: B. Yes

Sharks technically can be albino or leucistic. Albinism is defined by the lack of melanin pigment, while leucism describes loss or partial loss of multiple pigments. Albino or leucistic sharks have been spotted before, though it's extremely rare since their discoloring makes them stick out to both their preys and predators.

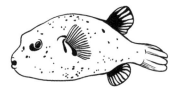

9. The bottom-dwelling wobbegong, whose name is believed to come from the Australian Aborigine word for "shaggy beard," is a type of shark that resembles a flat Muppet with intricate yarny, branch-like lobes along its jaws. What is this shaggy beard used for?

A. A disguise, along with its camouflage coloring, to blend in better with rocks

B. A filter to sift through sand and grit for small crustaceans

C. A net: the lobe secretes a sticky substance to trap small fish

ANSWER: A. A disguise

In addition to the wobbegong's camo-patterned skin, its mouth tassels look like seaweed and coral, thus helping the shark blend even more effectively among its sand and rock surroundings. The wobbegong is one of the most impressive ambush hunters among sharks, using its plain-looking tail to trick prey into thinking that it's just a normal fish hanging out among corals and seaweed. Goofy name, serious business.

10. What is the snout of the shark called?

A. Rostrum, like a squid's beak

B. Proboscis, like a butterfly's mouth tube

C. Muzzle, like a dog's nose

# ANSWER: A. Rostrum

Rostrum also describes the saw part of a sawfish, the nose of a dolphin, and the sword part of a marlin. Despite so many dog-related terms describing sharks, this one goes to the fish.

11. Sharks sure can smell, but how good are they at listening?

A. Pretty good, actually

B. Not great

ANSWER: A. Pretty good

Despite not having recognizable ears outside of their bodies, sharks do have a hole on the side of each eye that connects right into their inner ears. Sound travels faster underwater (about 4.5 times faster than on land) so sharks are able to detect prey activity up to 800 feet away.

12. If you ever stumbled upon a rotting shark corpse, the smell will most likely remind you of what?

A. Rotten eggs—sulfuric smell

B. Farts—methane smell

C. Harsh cleaning agents—ammonia smell

ANSWER: C. Harsh cleaning agents

In order for sharks to achieve a similar ion concentration in their bodies to seawater to maintain balance, they rely on a high urea concentration in their blood. Their kidneys reabsorb large amounts of urea from their own shark pee. When sharks die, the urea in their bodies will break down into ammonia, and the smell is quite chemically harsh and gag-inducing.

13. *Your eyes are feeling heavy...you are getting sleepy...*Believe it or not, some sharks can be hypnotized. When the side of their heads get rubbed, some sharks will flip onto their backs and get sent into a natural state of paralysis for about 15 minutes. What is this phenomenon called?

A. Vasovagal response

B. Torpor

C. Tonic immobility

ANSWER: C. Tonic immobility

Marine biologists will often exploit this natural response when studying or tagging sharks, though no one knows for sure why this happens in sharks—it may be for mating or for playing dead, like in other animal species. However, there have been recorded accounts of killer whales using this trick to subdue sharks for food. In 1997, it was documented that a female orca induced tonic immobility on a great white shark, and then proceeded to feast on shark parts. Vasovagal response is a technical term for fainting, and torpor is a slowed metabolism state that's similar to hibernation.

14. In an average 6-foot-tall human adult, the combined length of both the small and large intestine is around 25 feet. About how long is the intestine of a 6-foot-long shark?

A. 1 foot

B. 25 feet

C. 40 feet

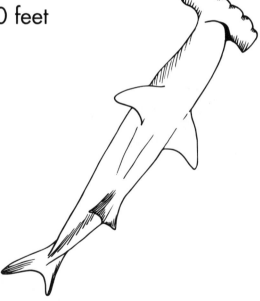

ANSWER: A. 1 foot

Despite the short length, the shark intestine can absorb and digest a lot thanks to the intestine's series of internal folds or valves, which greatly increase surface area for absorption. There are three basic types of internal valves: ring (imagine a newly opened package tray of stacked Samoas Girl Scout Cookies), spiral (imagine the curliest curly fry), or scroll (imagine a roll of paper towels). The surface area inside a shark's intestine can sometimes be four times larger than the surface area of a human intestine!

15. Here's a brainbuster: do sharks sleep?

A. Yeah, no.

B. No, yeah.

C. These answer options are terrible.

ANSWER: ALL OF THE ABOVE

Congratulations, you've stumbled on the only real trick question in this book! We know so much about sharks, but there's so much more that we just don't know for sure due to the myriad of shark species and the fact that dedicated shark research has only existed for a few decades. Long story short: It is entirely up to how "sleep" is defined, but we do know that for sharks, it comes down to breathing. Sharks get oxygen from the water that flows over their gills. If they stop swimming, then technically, there's no oxygen going into their bodies. It's a common myth that sharks don't sleep because they have to be constantly moving. Some species of shark go on autopilot and still swim and move, but their brains seem to be in an unconscious state. Some sharks rest by staying still and using spiracles, small holes by their eyes that connect to their mouths, to supply oxygen. In the bizarre case of the Cave of Sleeping Sharks in Mexico, divers found piles of reef sharks lying motionless, almost trance-like. Experts surmised that the water in this sea cave is probably extra oxygenated. So sharks do rest, but whether or not they're asleep is not definite.

16. The crested bullhead shark has pink teeth! How on earth did that happen?

A. Their tooth enamel is almost transparent, so the pinkish tint is actually from the blood vessels.

B. The enamel coating of their teeth contains the pigment carotenoid, which has a reddish hue.

C. They munch on red sea urchins that dye their teeth pink.

ANSWER: C. They munch on red sea urchins.

The cute bottom-dwelling crested bullhead shark (named for the dinosaur-like ridges above their eyes) has a pretty specialized diet of mostly sea urchins that have red chromophores in their urchin spines. However, the crested bullhead shark is known to also feast on egg cases of the Port Jackson shark, chewing through the leathery capsule and then sucking and slurping the nutrient-rich eggs down. It's a shark-eat-shark world, man.

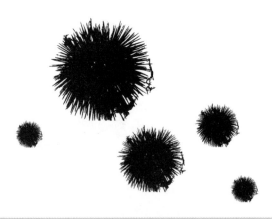

17. The eel-like and jawless hagfish has quite the secret weapon when dealing with hungry predatory sharks. When threatened, the hagfish will deter the shark by doing what?

A. Tying its extremely flexible, rope-like body around the shark's head and snout

B. Secreting a slime that clogs up the shark's gills

C. Zapping the shark with an electrical charge that disorients the shark's electrosensory organ

ANSWER: B. Secreting a slime

The hagfish is a weird, weird, weird kind of fish: it is finless and scaleless, has one nostril, and has poor vision due to its non-compound eyes. It seems like it would be the ideal easy meal for sharks...except for the slime. Oh, *so much* slime! One hagfish can unload enough mucus to fill up a 5-gallon container! When a shark's got a hagfish in its mouth, the hagfish goo will clog shark gills, causing the shark to choke and convulse, and eventually let the captured hagfish go. *But wouldn't the hagfish choke on its own secretion?* Yes, it could, but the hagfish is able to knot itself and move the knot along its body to "scrape off" the slime!

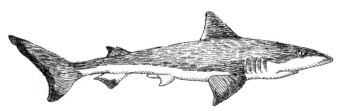

18. Poor Greenland shark, it's practically blind thanks to:

A. Parasitic crustaceans that specifically latch onto the shark's eyes and destroy the cornea.

B. The urea content in their body is so high that it slows the nervous system down.

C. Mother Nature—they're born that way.

ANSWER: A. Parasitic crustaceans

The inch-long parasite just *dangles* from the Greenland shark's eyeball, like a suction cup made up of nightmares. If it makes you feel better, the Greenland shark is not as dependent on sight as it is on smell. Since they seek out extremely cold water, Greenland sharks swim in the very dark depths of the ocean.

19. Can't really see in murky or dark waters? No problem. Sharks have an electrosensory organ in their heads called ampullae of Lorenzini that helps them pick up on small electrical signals generated from muscle movements of other organisms swimming in the water. In addition to having a strange name, the organ also looks pretty strange: a clear substance with a texture that resembles what condiment?

A. Mayonnaise—slippery, oily cream

B. Marmalade—globular jelly

C. Vegemite—viscous paste

ANSWER: B. Marmalade

The pores around the shark's head are actually filled with this jelly stuff, and this sensitive substance is all connected by a network of nerves that relays electric field information back to the shark brain, essentially drawing out a map of electric activity allowing the shark to "see" its surroundings. Spidey sense? More like *sharkey sense*!

SAY WHAT?

Sharks have body parts with functions that are as delightfully weird as their names. From head to tail and the whole finchilada, here are some interesting names of shark organs and parts. Test your etymology skills and anatomy know-how by matching the name of the body part to its corresponding function.

A. Barbel

B. Claspers

C. Cloaca

D. Nictitating membrane

E. Spiracle

F. *Tapetum lucidum*

G. Tesserae

1. Like cats and dogs, sharks too have a reflective surface in their eyes that makes their eyes shine green in the dark, right behind their retinas. This tissue reflects visible light back through the retina to give sharks better night vision.

BODY PART: _____

2. This organ's name actually means "sewer" in Latin. And rightly so–it's the chamber in the shark where all the urinary, intestinal, and genital tracts lead and open to. Reptiles and birds also share the same "expelling system," where the animal's feces and urine are all mixed up and exit out from one hole. For birds, the waste lands on your car; for sharks, it blooms out into a puffy yellowing cloud in the water then quickly dissipates.

BODY PART: _____

3. Having a skeleton made up of cartilage is important for sharks because cartilage is less dense and weighs less than bone, thus helping sharks save energy. On locations where sharks use the most force, like their backbone for swimming and jaws for biting, the cartilage is covered with this—a special lining that's made up of tiny calcium crystals providing extra support and fortification that's strong like bone.

BODY PART: _____

4. This part of the shark is a slit or a hole that's located by the eye (not to be confused with the shark "ear," which is another hole). It supplies oxygen directly to the shark's brain and serves as a backup gill when the shark's mouth is preoccupied with eating. Ground-loving bottom-dwelling sharks also use this to breathe since their gills get too close to the sandy, gritty ocean floor.

BODY PART: _____

5. The easiest way to describe this body part is that it's the shark penis...es. Located behind their pelvic fin, these organs are used to penetrate into the female to deliver semen. And they do come in a pair, though only one is inserted into the lady shark. Though they function like a penis, these organs are not independent appendages, but more like extensions of the pelvic fin.

BODY PART: _____

6. Though it sounds like something sharks do at the gym to get swole, this body part is a sensory organ around the mouth. Found on catfish, kois, and some species of sharks, they're used to help search for food in dark waters and along the ocean floor, and described often as being like "fish whiskers."

BODY PART: _____

7. Often referred to as "the third eyelid," this body part covers and helps to protect shark eyeballs during hunting or in the event of an attack. Even though not all sharks have this extra protection, the shark body will do almost everything to protect the precious eyeball: the great white shark will roll their eyes backward when striking prey.

BODY PART: _____

# ANSWER:

1. F. *Tapetum lucidum*
   (Latin for "bright tapestry")

2. C. Cloaca

3. G. Tesserae

4. E. Spiracle

5. B. Claspers

6. A. Barbel

7. D. Nictitating membrane

NIFTY SHADES OF GRAY

Time to turn down the lights and see if you can satisfy these burning questions about shark reproduction and makin' babies. Barry White optional.

1. Love sure hurts for female blue sharks, since their mating ritual involves some biting from their suitors. So female blue sharks have developed what to combat these *love nibbles*?

A. More flexible skeletons to twist out of a bite grip

B. Smelly gland secretions to ward off the male

C. Extremely thick skin

ANSWER: C. Extremely thick skin

Female blue sharks have skin that is three times thicker than that of their fellow dudes. And a bite mark on a female is one of the notable ways to tell the genders apart.

2. Sometimes, a gal's just not interested and needs to swipe left. What do female sharks do if they are unwilling to mate?

A. Close up their cloaca muscles to deny male entry

B. Bite back to show disinterest and aggression

C. Hang out in shallow waters

ANSWER: C. Hang out in shallow waters

The female shark often mates with many different suitors during mating season; however, on the rare occasion that she chooses not to mate, she will spend some quality time alone in shallow waters to make it difficult to mate with her. The shallow depth makes it tricky for males to flip her over for sex, and the female can easily push her cloaca against the sea floor to deny penetration.

3. Awww, look at the cute baby shark, which is also called what mainly mammalian name?

A. Cub—ferocious animal like a lion, bear, or tiger

B. Kit—fast and sneaky animal like a fox, or weasel

C. Pup—canine animal like a dog, coyote, or wolf

ANSWER: C. Pup

Until the 16th century, seafarers referred to sharks as "sea dogs." Now, who's a good boy?

4. True or false: Sharks do not take care of their young when they are born.

A. True, shark pups are on their own right after birth.

B. False, the nurse shark stays close to her pups, hence the name.

ANSWER: A. True

It's a hard-knock life for shark pups–they're on their own since day one. And as for nurse sharks, they do not nurse or look after their young. No one really knows where the name comes from. The prevalent theory is that it came from "hurse," an Old English name for sea-floor sharks, but a cuter theory is that the fish makes sucking sounds like a nursing baby.

5. Baby sand sharks are known for adelphophagy, which sounds like a boring word for what utterly captivating phenomenon?

A. Knowing when to leave the womb after exactly 300 days—named so like Oracle of Delphi

B. Eating their siblings in the womb—named so like a fraternity

C. Being raised by dolphins after birth—named so like *delfina*, dolphin in Italian

ANSWER: B. Eating their siblings

Isn't Mother Nature impressive yet horrifying? Often, the larger and more developed sand shark babies are known to eat their own siblings in the womb for nutrients. *Adelphi* is the Greek word for siblings. Some species of sharks commit oophagy (which is less intense), where developing embryos feed on unfertilized eggs in the uterus.

6. Hold up, let's take a second to clear the air: Do sharks lay eggs or do they give birth to live young?

A. They lay eggs like fish do!

B. They give birth like dolphins do!

C. Uh…both!

ANSWER: C. Both!

Out of the myriad of shark species, some sharks give live birth, some sharks lay eggs, and some sharks are kind of in between. Viviparous sharks like hammerheads and salmon sharks get pregnant and develop babies in the womb, complete with placenta and umbilical cord, not unlike humans. Their babies are born live. Oviparous sharks are similar to chickens in that they lay fertilized eggs that will eventually hatch. And remember the sibling-eating shark pups? That is an example of ovoviviparity, where the babies develop in the womb but without a placenta, so they need to eat their siblings or eggs for nutrients.

7. Even sharks have a taste for drama! It was almost like love at first sight for Leonie the zebra shark and her male partner at the ReefHQ aquarium in Queensland, Australia, when they first met in 1999. After living together and having several litters of pups, Leonie and her beau were then separated into different tanks in 2012, and Leonie has lived alone ever since. But in 2016, Leonie miraculously produced three babies. How on earth did this happen?!

A. Leonie kept a secret stash of sperm stored in her body to allow her to reproduce at will.

B. Leonie is hermaphroditic and has both male and female sexual organs.

C. Leonie indeed had virgin births and basically cloned herself.

 **A**NSWER: C. Leonie had virgin births and reproduced asexually.

Though extremely rare, female sharks in captivity have been known to reproduce without male partners. This type of asexual reproduction is known as parthenogenesis. When scientists examined Leonie's pups with DNA analysis, they found that the pups only had cells and genetic information from Leonie. When Leonie's living situation changed, she adapted, and *well, life finds a way*.

8. Think being pregnant for nine months is rough? How long is the average gestation period for sharks?

A. 12 months

B. 18 months

C. 24 months

ANSWER: C. 24 months

TWO YEARS! And that's the *average*! Some sharks, like the freaky nightmare-mouth frilled shark, can carry their young for up to three and a half years. That's almost someone's undergraduate college career.

CRYPTOQUOTE
PART 2

Ready to do some more decoding work? This is an encrypted quote about shark reproduction. Each letter stands for another. Try to look for certain letter patterns like single letters by themselves, and contractions. Unused letters are noted as well.

PUZZLE LETTER = ANSWER LETTER

A =

B =

C =

D =

E =

F =

G =

H = not used

I =

J =

K =

L =

M =

N =

O =

P =

Q =

R =

S =

T = not used

U = not used

V = not used

W =

X =

Y =

Z =

"NXN AZM RLZY GDFG QFRZ
"___ ___ ____ ____ ____

IDFBR JCGMICI CFG CFED
_____ _____ ___ ____

ZGDCB XL GDC YZQS?...
_____ __ ___ ____?...

XG'I GBMC. ZLKA EFLLXSFK
__,_ ____. ____ _____

JCGMICI IMBWXWC GZ SC
_____ _____ __ __

SZBL. EFL AZM XQFPXLC XJ
____. ___ ___ _____ __

OCZOKC YCBC KXRC GDFG?"
_____ ____ ____ ____?"

—Laini Taylor, author of the young adult fantasy series,
Daughter of Smoke and Bone

ANSWER:

A = Y	J = F	S = B
B = R	K = L	T = not used
C = E	L = N	U = not used
D = H	M = U	V = not used
E = C	N = D	W = V
F = A	O = P	X = I
G = T	P = G	Y = W
H = not used	Q = M	Z = O
I = S	R = K	

"DID YOU KNOW THAT MAKO SHARK FETUSES EAT EACH OTHER IN THE WOMB?… IT'S TRUE. ONLY CANNIBAL FETUSES SURVIVE TO BE BORN. CAN YOU IMAGINE IF PEOPLE WERE LIKE THAT?"

—Laini Taylor, author of the young adult fantasy series, *Daughter of Smoke and Bone*

3

HEY
CHUMS!
RELATIONSHIP
WITH HUMANS

IT'S TIME TO
TEST THE WATERS

Sharks had been swimming in Earth's waters 400 million years before humans came into the scene. There's no doubt humans have developed a rich history and fascination with these fish. Take this quiz to see how much you know about the relationship between us humans and sharks, and how much our presence affects theirs.

1. What exactly is "chum"?

A. Shark poop

B. Random fish parts

C. A group of sharks during feeding time

ANSWER: B. Random fish parts

Chum is a mixture of ground-up fish parts, blood, and bone that fishermen use to attract sharks (and other fish) since sharks have an amazing sense of smell. The practice of chumming, or scattering chum into water, is actually prohibited in a lot of areas, mainly because of the dangers of conditioning sharks to associate humans with their food. And though it's the same word, the friend version of the word "chum" comes from a shortened version of "chamber fellow."

2. What is the official name of someone who studies sharks?

A. Aggroichthyologist

B. Sharkist

C. Shark biologist

ANSWER: C. Shark biologist

It's definitely not the most exotic answer, but shark biologists (or elasmobranchologists, a term that is not really used anymore) are widely respected for their hard work in marine biology due to the difficulties caused by reduced population of sharks in the world.

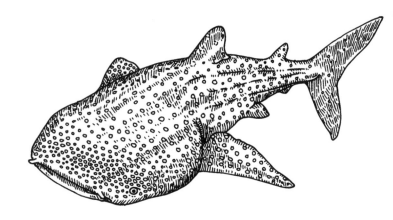

3. Chef and famous foodie Anthony Bourdain once described this traditional shark meat dish as "the single worst, most disgusting and terrible tasting thing." What did he eat, and from where?

A. Shark fin soup from Hong Kong

B. Pickled dogfish from the United Kingdom

C. Cured shark jerky from Iceland

ANSWER: C. Cured shark jerky

Though all of the answer options are real dishes, the Icelandic national dish of *Kæstur hákarl* made of the Greenland shark is notorious for its extremely fishy and strong, gag-inducing ammonia flavor. After being gutted and beheaded, the shark body is buried underground to ferment and rot for a few months, then hung to dry. Definitely not for the faint of heart (or stomach).

4. Shark finning is a controversial practice that is banned in many countries. What is shark finning technically?

A. Buying and selling of shark fins, now causing a huge illegal operation

B. Serving shark fin soup in restaurants

C. Cutting all the fins off of a shark at sea and throwing the shark body back into water

ANSWER: C. Cutting all the fins off, then discarding body

The sharks are often still alive when finners slice off all of their fins, the most expensive and valuable part of a shark. They sink to the bottom of the ocean because they cannot swim without their fins. The sharks usually die from asphyxiation since they require mass quantities of moving water (from swimming) to breathe. Sharks are heavy and take up a lot of space, so when finning is done out at sea, fisherman don't need to haul the entire fish, just the valuable fins. The practice of finning is illegal in many countries. And some countries, like Australia, have regulations that require fishermen to carry the entire shark with fins attached in order to decrease finning at sea.

5. Commercially available chemical shark repellent deters sharks by smelling like what?

A. Dead sharks

B. Burnt chemicals

C. Killer whales

ANSWER: A. Dead sharks

Well, it makes a whole lot of sense that sharks don't like going to areas that smell like their dead brethren! The practice of using dead sharks to repel live ones is an old seafaring lifehack shared by many old fishing cultures from around the world. A more recent method of shark repellent uses an electrochemical reaction to produce voltage to overwhelm a shark's sensory organs.

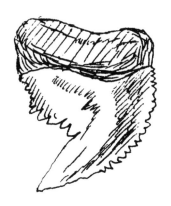

6. Great whites are notoriously difficult to retain in captivity due to their size, their need to travel long distances and have a constant flow of water to breathe, and their predatory nature of catching live food. What is the longest record for a white shark to survive in captivity?

A. 3 days at the Okinawa Churaumi Aquarium

B. 16 days at SeaWorld San Diego

C. 198 days at the Monterey Bay Aquarium

ANSWER: C. 198 days

Actually, all those answer options are from real instances of white shark captivities. Great whites would often refuse food when captured, and would die from malnutrition and stress. Back in 2004, the Monterey Bay Aquarium successfully kept their shark in captivity but released her back into the wild after 198 days, as she was causing trouble with other sharks in her tank.

7. Introduced to King Louis XV during the 18th century, *galuchat* is a luxury item made of what shark part?

A. Teeth

B. Skin

C. Eggs

ANSWER: B. Skin

Jean-Claude Galluchat, King Louis XV's master leatherworker, used shark and ray skins to craft luxury goods like furniture and fancy jewelry boxes. When sanded down, the micro-protrusions on the skin (dermal denticles) form an intricate bubbly mosaic pattern. First uses of shark skin even date back to 8th century Japan, when it was used for armor and sword sheaths!

8. It's an island tradition to hang jars and bottles containing shark liver oil outside of many houses in Bermuda. What are these jars used for?

A. Good luck charms—the shark liver oil is believed to serve as a barrier from evil spirits coming through the door.

B. Storm indicators—the oil changes color when turbulent weather is approaching.

C. Bug catchers—the oil attracts and traps flying insects and palmetto bugs.

ANSWER: B. Storm indicator

It's simple: clear oil means clear skies, cloudy oil means a storm's brewin'. Before the time of mechanical or digital weather forecasting devices, Bermudans discovered this magical-seeming property of shark oil and found a way to make these "shark oil barometers." How and why does it work? The prevalent theory is that the electric charges in the air affect the oil. It's the shark body's own way of telling itself to go in deeper water when a storm is approaching!

9. What city is named "The Shark Tooth Capital of the World" due to the high amount of fossilized shark teeth that can be found on its shores?

A. Coffs Harbour, Australia

B. Carpinteria, California

C. Venice Beach, Florida

ANSWER: C. Venice Beach, Florida

Fossil collectors and shark enthusiasts even gather for the official Venice Beach Shark Tooth Festival held every spring!

10. Which US president signed the Shark Conservation Act into law?

A. Barack Obama

B. George W. Bush

C. Bill Clinton

ANSWER: A. Barack Obama

Shark finning was already illegal in US waters but it only applied to fishing boats, so non-fishing boats were able to transport and transship shark fins. The Shark Conservation Act closed the loophole and made it illegal for non-fishing boats to transport shark fins.

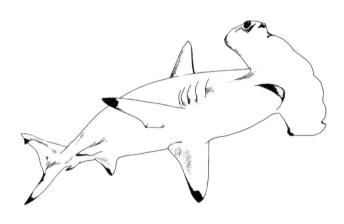

11. In Australia, the term "flake" is used to describe what shark-related thing?

A. Surfer term for scars from common small shark bites

B. Shark teeth found on beaches

C. Shark meat for eating

ANSWER: C. Shark meat for eating

Thanks to its mild fish flavor, ready supply, and lack of fish bones (since sharks are cartilaginous!), flake has become a common type of fish to be used in Australian fish and chip shops. Flake comes from a variety of Australian sharks like the wobbegong and the gummy shark; the latter is named not for its texture, but for its seemingly toothless appearance due to inward-facing teeth.

12. For centuries, sailors and scientists have witnessed the extraordinary relationship between the black-and-white banded pilot fish and the oceanic whitetip shark. The pilot fish tidies up the shark from parasites, and in exchange, the shark looks like a bodyguard to the smaller fish. In biology, this is known as a:

A. Parasitic relationship

B. Mutualistic relationship

C. Commensal relationship

ANSWER: C. Mutualistic relationship

In mutualistic relationships, both parties benefit from each other (parasitic: one party is benefited by harming the other; commensal: one party is benefited without affecting the other). Seafarers once believed that pilot fish would guide ships to land.

13. You might not find shark on the menu, but you're more likely to find shark in what part of a sushi restaurant?

A. On the prep table

B. Near the bathrooms

C. By the window

ANSWER: A. On the prep table

Oroshiki is a type of extremely fine grater that's lined with shark skin and exclusively used for grating real wasabi in professional sushi restaurants. The sandpaper-like quality yields a super smooth and velvety wasabi texture.

14. In 2004, shark biologists tracked a great white shark that completed the first documented round-trip ocean crossing, shattering the record for the farthest distance traveled ever by a shark. About how long was her swim?

A. Up and down the Amazon river once

B. 75 marathons

C. Almost the circumference of Mars

ANSWER: C. Almost the circumference of Mars

The shark swam from Africa to Australia and back in nine months, traveling a total of 12,400 miles. (A lap in the Amazon is about 9,000 miles, 75 marathons is nearly 2,000 miles, and the circumference of Mars is around 13,000 miles.) The great white shark was named "Nicole" in honor of Aussie actress Nicole Kidman.

15. Ya better watch out! There are also poisonous and venomous sharks. Which of the following statements is true?

A. Greenland sharks are poisonous; dogfish are venomous.

B. Dogfish are poisonous; Greenland sharks are venomous.

C. Both terms mean the same thing.

ANSWER: A. Greenland sharks are poisonous; dogfish are venomous.

What's the difference between an animal that is poisonous and an animal that is venomous? Venomous animals must inflict a wound, like a snake bite or a scorpion sting, in order to deliver toxins. And things that are poisonous deliver toxins by touch or by being consumed, like the belladonna nightshade or some species of frogs. Thanks to their extremely high urea content, Greenland shark flesh is poisonous to humans and must be boiled and prepared through and through before consumption. And dogfish have dorsal spines that are covered with venom (though it's only mildly toxic to humans).

16. The fear of sharks is known as what?

A. Lamniphobia

B. Squaliphobia

C. Galeophobia

ANSWER: C. Galeophobia

Though the Latin term *lamnia* is attributed to sharks,
phobia words stem from the Greek language and *galeos*
is the Greek root for sharks.

STORY TIME AROUND THE WORLD

For centuries, sharks have inspired cultures around the world with their mysterious, splendid (and sometimes dangerous) appeal. These wonderful creatures have been woven into rich stories and myths as vengeful gods, protectors of oceans, and wily tricksters, and have captured the imaginations of many seafaring and oceanic nations and tribes. Let's take a trip around the world, and see if you can match the nation with its cultural shark myth.

NATIONS & CULTURES:

BRAZIL

FIJI

GREECE

HAWAII

INUIT

NEW ZEALAND (MAORI)

ZANZIBAR (TANZANIA)

1. **The Change of Heart.** Both feared and revered, Dakuwaqa was a protector god who was half shark, half man. Dakuwaqa found himself in an enraged battle against an octopus river goddess after an attempt to conquer Kadavu Island. Dakuwaqa admitted defeat after getting all his teeth pulled and vowed to protect Kadavu instead. Dakuwaqa protected local fishermen from evil spirits and ensured plentiful bounty.

NATION: _____

2. **Never Upset the In-Laws!** Celebrated hunter Nohi-Abassi was not happy with his mother-in-law, so he came up with a plan of training a shark to eat and kill her. Turns out, mom found out about this, so she secretly disguised her daughter as the trained shark. When Nohi-Abassi let the (disguised) shark loose, the shark attacked Nohi-Abassi instead and scattered his bitten remains into the heavens among the stars. His decapitated leg became the constellation we now know as Orion's Belt.

NATION: _____

3. The Classic Animal Switcheroo.

Kawariki was the daughter of a powerful tribal healer, raised by her protective father to become the future leader of their tribe. Kawariki was promised to a notable man of another tribe through an arranged marriage, but she fell in love with Tutira, one of her childhood friends. After discovering the lovebirds, Kawariki's father turned Tutira into a shark. As Kawariki cried, her tears had a magical effect on Tutira, allowing him to take on human form once every month so the two could continue to meet in secret. When a huge tsunami hit their village and swept the tribespeople out to danger in the sea, Tutira used his shark form to rescue people. As an apology and as an act of gratitude, Kawariki's father reversed the curse and gave his blessing to the couple in love. Everyone loves a happy ending!

NATION: _____

4. Ah, Cannibalism. Lamia, the beautiful queen of Libya, was one of the (many) mistresses of a great god whose wife erupted with jealousy and wanted revenge. So Lamia's children were taken from her and were subsequently killed. Filled with grief, Lamia lost her mind and went mad. She started stealing other people's children and ate them. Lamia then transformed into a giant shark creature and continued her crazy, vengeful ways of devouring innocent children.

NATION: _____

5. Highfalutin. Ka'ahupahau was a goddess born in human form with beautiful red hair. She was later turned into a sacred shark who lived in the waters near her family. She was fed kava, a plant with drug-like properties believed to have magical and healing properties, and in turn, she would protect humans from other sharks.

NATION: _____

6. Joke's on You, LOL. Once a hungry shark spotted a monkey living in a fruit tree, and asked if the monkey would help him eat food by picking some

fruit off the tree. As payment, the shark offered to take the monkey on his back to a great feast. While riding together, the monkey discovered that the shark had an ulterior motive: the shark needed a monkey heart to cure his king's illness. The monkey counter-tricked the shark by announcing that he left his own heart back at the tree and needed to doubleback to get it. Once they got back to the same tree, the monkey jumped off to safety.

NATION: _____

7. **Urine It for Good Now.** When young Sedna broke the news to her father that she wanted to marry a bird, he killed the bird and threw Sedna into the sea from a kayak. As she clung to the side of the boat, he sliced off each of her fingers until she lost her grip. (So intense!) The waters swallowed Sedna and she became the Mother of the Sea. Her decapitated digits became various mammals of the sea, and she befriended a Greenland shark who promised to avenge her. The shark lived in Sedna's urine pot, and eventually did kill and eat Sedna's father when he was out fishing at sea.

NATION: _____

ANSWER:

1. Fiji

2. Brazil

3. New Zealand (Maori)

4. Greece (The unnamed great god was Zeus. Would've been too easy!)

5. Hawaii

6. Zanzibar (Tanzania)

7. Inuit

CRYPTOQUOTE
PART 3

Time for another brain-sweating cryptographic puzzle! Here we have a quote from Jaws himself, but it's all encrypted! Each letter stands for another. Try to look for certain letter patterns: single letters by themselves are probably an A, contractions usually are -'RE, -'NT, or -'VE, and, of course, the word "SHARK" appears a few times. Unused letters are noted as well.

PUZZLE LETTER = ANSWER LETTER

A = not used

B =

C =

D =

E =

F =

G =

H =

I = not used

J =

K =

L =

M =

N = not used

O =

P =

Q =

R =

S = not used

T = not used

U =

V = not used

W =

X =

Y =

Z =

"LW ZPYRYDW H XJHPD

WRWPB GKFW LW WMGWP

GJW LHGWP LJWPW XJHPDX

JHZZWM GY UW, OYP LW

OYPEWG: GJW YQWHM KX

MYG YCP GWPPKGYPB —

KG'X GJWKPX."

—Peter Benchley, author of *Jaws*
and cowriter of the film adaptation

ANSWER:

A = not used

B = Y

C = U

D = K

E = G

F = M

G = T

H = A

I = not used

J = H

K = I

L = W

M = N

N = not used

O = F

P = R

Q = C

R = V

S = not used

T = not used

U = B

V = not used

W = E

X = S

Y = O

Z = P

"WE PROVOKE A SHARK EVERY TIME WE ENTER THE WATER WHERE SHARKS HAPPEN TO BE, FOR WE FORGET: THE OCEAN IS NOT OUR TERRITORY— IT'S THEIRS."

—Peter Benchley, author of *Jaws* and cowriter of the film adaptation

THE DOS AND DON'TS OF SURVIVING A SHARK ATTACK

Even though the odds of being attacked by a shark are about 1 in 11.5 million, one can never be too prepared. But with so many old wives' tales and shark attack misconceptions, what exactly are the dos and don'ts when facing a potentially dangerous shark encounter? Here are 10 common pieces of advice about surviving a shark attack. Half of them consist of sound advice and half of them are, well, debated, ineffective, or even dangerous. Circle either DO or DON'T and see just how shark savvy you are. YOLO!

BEFORE GOING INTO THE WATER:

1. DO DON'T
   ...wear bright colors to avoid looking like fish.

2. DO DON'T
   ...swim when it's light outside.

3. DO DON'T
   ...avoid swimming near fishing boats.

IF A SHARK IS APPROACHING YOU FROM A DISTANCE:

4. DO   DON'T
   ...float and play dead.

5. DO   DON'T
   ...keep eye contact.

6. DO   DON'T
   ...find something solid to back up on.

7. DO   DON'T
   ...use freestyle stroke to swim.

IF A SHARK IS ATTACKING YOU:

8. DO DON'T
   ...punch the nose.

9. DO DON'T
   ...keep quiet.

10. DO DON'T
    ...fight.

ANSWER:

Before diving into the correct answers, the important factor to consider during a shark attack is not necessarily *what* to do, but *when* to do. Sharks are hunters, and thus follow a pattern of stages during an attack; the best way to think about dealing with a potentially attacking shark is to react accordingly to these stages.

Before going into the water, make sure you're swimming under good conditions.

1. **DON'T** wear bright colors to avoid looking like fish.

Divers and surfers suggest not to wear "yum yum yellow." Sharks may not be able to distinguish color, but they sure can see contrast underwater. Colors like yellow and orange will stand out to a shark. Some shark experts even note that swimsuit tan lines will be enough contrast to pique interest. Also, avoid wearing anything shiny like jewelry or watches because the reflections on the bling might look like fish scales shimmering in the water.

2. **DO** swim when it's light outside.

Never swim under conditions that impair your (and a shark's) field of vision, like when it's dark during early morning or night time. This also applies to swimming in murky waters, which may increase the likelihood of a shark encounter.

3. **DO** avoid swimming near fishing boats.

Sure, there's safety in numbers, but not when there's a free-for-all shark buffet around you. The smell of fish parts and fish activity around fishing boats is like ringing the supper bell for sharks. And, related to this, avoid swimming in areas where there are dolphins and seagulls, because they often look for the same prey for food (in addition of being prime shark food themselves.)

If you see a shark approaching from a distance, stay calm and defensive, and do not attract attention. Humans cannot outswim a shark.

4. **DON'T** float and play dead.

At this distance, you want to appear to be something either not interesting to a shark or something not worth its time. Playing dead doesn't do anything but attract attention and make you seem like easy prey.

5. **DO** keep eye contact.

Different shark species have different ways of assessing or potentially attacking. Some are ambush hunters, some come straight on, and some might not even be interested in you. Regardless of the shark type, always keep watch of the animal as it approaches.

6. **DO** find something solid to back up on.

Sharks circle and find angles, so the space behind you is your biggest vulnerability. If you're close to a reef, an outcropping of rocks, or any solid obstruction, then try to slowly move and back up onto it to limit the shark's possible angles for attack.

7. **DON'T** use freestyle stroke to swim.

Swim only if you're close to shore or close to something solid to back up on to. And the ideal way to swim is smooth, quiet strokes to minimize the amount of thrashing and kicking. The preferred stroke is the reverse breaststroke because that way, you're able to keep an eye on the shark as well.

8. **DON'T** punch the nose.

If a shark is attacking you, it's time to get aggressive back. Punching the nose *is* effective, but the nose is unfortunately very close to the toothy maw of a shark. Unless you have a clear shot or have something solid with you that you can punch with (surfboard, pole, etc.), punching the nose is risky when there's all the splashing and thrashing going on. Do go for the sides and punch or scratch the eyes and gills. Obstructing the shark's eyesight and breathing will more likely deter the shark from further attacks.

9. **DON'T** keep quiet.

The more people are aware of your situation, the more likely you can get help.

10. **DO** fight.

The professional advice for those under a shark attack is when all else fails, go nuts as a last resort. If a shark is attacking you, fight back as hard and as aggressively as you can. Shout, elbow, kick, do whatever to hurt the shark enough for it to leave you alone. If the shark leaves, there's still a chance for it to come back after an attack. Swim smoothly to shore before the shark returns or, if you're wounded, get to shore before the blood attracts more sharks.

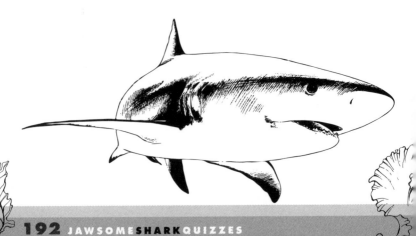

4

LIKE, TOTALLY JAWSOME!

SHARKS IN POP CULTURE

BITE DOWN ON THIS

Our fascination with sharks has jumped out of the water and into our lives, from Saturday morning cartoons to the world of professional golf. Put on your water skis and let's see if you can jump over these shark pop culture questions.

1. Shark Week is the Discovery Channel's annual television event when multiple original shows about sharks are aired to celebrate these awesome animals. It has now become a mega pop culture phenomenon. When did the first Shark Week hit the airwaves?

A. 1974

B. 1988

C. 2000

ANSWER: B. 1988

From its humble offering of a few shows during inaugural launch to its current chum-packed programming with celebrity hosts, Shark Week has become the longest running US cable TV programming event in history. Some of the past Shark Week hosts include *Jaws*' author Peter Benchley, actor Andy Samberg, *Mythbusters*' Adam Savage and Jamie Hyneman, and horror film director Eli Roth.

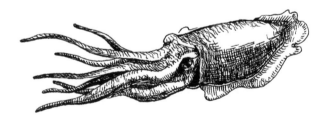

2. Before becoming a Batman villain living in Arkham Asylum, Warren White (aka the Great White Shark) had what former profession?

A. Businessman and financier

B. Mob boss operating under a fishery front

C. Gotham crime lab scientist

ANSWER: A. Businessman and financier

Warren White thought he was so clever for pleading insanity to avoid any prison sentence after embezzling tons of money from his company's pension fund. But White's plan backfired when he was sent to Arkham Asylum, where he was tortured by other Gotham villains. Killer Croc slashed his neck to give him gill-like scars, Mr. Freeze trapped him in his icy cell until his skin turned pale and his nose, hair, and lips froze off, gradually making Warren White look more and more like his namesake. He eventually snapped and embraced his new identity, and he even sharpened his own teeth to look more like the animal. Ah, fun times.

3. The term "card shark" describes either a card game cheater or an expert card player that takes advantage of less-skilled gamers. Where does the term come from?

A. Mangling of the word "sharp," meaning clever and skilled

B. German word *shurke*, meaning rascal

C. Actually describing the animal, as in the big ferocious fish at the table

ANSWER: B. German word *shurke*

Though the terms "card shark" and "card sharp" can be used interchangeably, the shark part of the phrase is believed to come from the German word for a roguish type of swindler.

4. The phrase "jumping the shark" is used to describe a moment when something that was once great has reached a low point in popularity or relevance, often marked by an over-the-top event to garner attention. This phrase came from what TV show that featured a character literally jumping over a shark?

A. *Happy Days*—While touring Los Angeles, Fonzie accepts a dare to jump over a shark.

B. *Charlie's Angels*—Model-turned-private-investigator and new Angel Jill jumps over shark-infested waters on a broken highway section in a car.

C. *The Beverly Hillbillies*—Jethro tries out his new jet ski, but strays too far away.

ANSWER: A. Happy Days

Actor Henry Winkler, who famously played Fonzie, was actually a skilled water-skier in real life. Despite the sheer gimmicky ridiculousness of this episode, *Happy Days* did continue to air for another seven years.

5. Kool-Aid once released a strawberry-orange-banana drink flavor, along with its very own flavor mascot: a pink shark under what literary punny name?

A. Sharklett O'Banana

B. Berry Sharkspeare

C. Sharkleberry Fin

 # ANSWER: C. Sharkleberry Fin

It's important to know that Sharkleberry Fin wears sunglasses.

6. The shark-faced Curtiss P-40 Warhawk aircraft is one of the most iconic and recognizable combat aircraft noses in history. The shark insignia was popularized by The Flying Tigers, who were all official members of what country's air force during the 1940s?

A. China

B. USA

C. Germany

ANSWER: A. China

Tricky, tricky! The Flying Tigers was the nickname for the First American Volunteer Group (AVG) of the Chinese Air Force. AVG consisted of recruited American pilot volunteers with the mission of helping China defend itself from the Imperial Japanese Army during World War II. Volunteers were from various branches of the US military but all members were officially recognized as members of the Chinese Air Force.

7. In the Harry Potter universe, which character gave himself a head of a shark?

A. George Weasley

B. Viktor Krum

C. Ron Weasley

ANSWER: B. Viktor Krum

In order to breathe underwater for a prolonged time in the second task in the Triwizard Cup tournament, competitor and Durmstrang student Viktor Krum went with a freaky shark head, whereas his competitors used gillyweed and bubblehead charms.

8. Former Houston Rockets player Yao Ming used to play for (then later bought) what local Chinese basketball club team?

A. Shanghai Sharks

B. Hong Kong Hammerheads

C. Beijing Bullsharks

ANSWER: A. Shanghai Sharks

The 7'6" wonder played for the Shanghai Sharks before his NBA career. When he learned that his former team was having financial troubles, he bought the team in 2009!

9. The US entrepreneurial hit reality show *Shark Tank* is actually based on what international show that sparked an entire investor-based TV show trend all over the world?

A. *Money Tigers* from Japan

B. *Dragon's Den* from the United Kingdom

C. *Lion's Mouth* from Finland

ANSWER: A. Money Tigers from Japan

Shark Tank, *Dragon's Den*, and *Lion's Mouth* are all localized versions of the original Japanese show that started it all. Versions of the *Money Tigers* have been produced in nearly 30 countries, many of them named after ferocious animals. As of 2016, the most successful and lucrative business that has come out of the American version of *Shark Tank* is the Scrub Daddy, a smiley-face polyurethane scratch-free super sponge that hardens in cold water and softens in hot water.

10. "We're gonna need a bigger boat." This iconic quote from the 1979 blockbuster *Jaws* is listed in the American Film Institute's 100 Greatest Movie Quotes of All Time.

A. True

B. False

ANSWER: B. False

Sorry! This is a bit of a trick question; this is a common misquote. The correct line is, "*You're* gonna need a bigger boat." Other victims of misquotation include: "Luke, I am your father," (real version: "No, I am your father") from *The Empire Strikes Back*; "Mirror, mirror, on the wall..." (real version: "Magic mirror, on the wall...") from *Snow White*; and "Hello, Clarice," (real version: "Good evening, Clarice") from *Silence of the Lambs*. As for the actual *Jaws'* boat quote, that sits quite snugly in the thirty-fifth spot of the greatest movie quotes list.

11. Bryan Gaw made a huge splash when he danced seemingly out of sync in a cartoonish shark suit at Katy Perry's Super Bowl halftime show, and was affectionately named by the public as "Left Shark." Which Super Bowl did Left Shark made his debut?

A. Super Bowl XLVIII, 2014, East Rutherford, NJ

B. Super Bowl XLIX, 2015, Glendale, AZ

C. Super Bowl 50, 2016, Santa Clara, CA

ANSWER: B. Super Bowl XLIX, 2015, Glendale, AZ

Other featured performers Katy brought on stage include Lenny Kravitz and Missy Elliot, but it was really Left Shark that became a cultural phenomenon.

12. Two university professors invented a machine (dubbed The Gene-Slammer) that can change aquatic animals into human hybrids. This is the premise of what shark-centric cartoon series?

A. Street Sharks

B. TigerSharks

C. Jabberjaw

ANSWER: A. Street Sharks

The show ran from 1994 to 1997, and the main characters were the four Bolton brothers who could transform into four different types of sharks: Ripster the great white, Jab the hammerhead, Streex the tiger shark, and Big Slammu the whale shark.

LAMIA NAMIA MANIA

Sharks are not only fearsome sea creatures, they are also fierce competitors in a variety of professional sports–when a player is named after one! Each of the following professional athletes is nicknamed "Shark." Can you match the person with the sport they are known for playing?

Jerry Tarkanian	Poker
Jeff Samardzija	Professional wrestling
Greg Norman	Basketball
Humberto Brenes	Snooker and pool
Kenneth Gant	Golf
Mark Shrader	Baseball
Mark Selby	American football

ANSWER:

JERRY TARKANIAN, a.k.a. "Tark the Shark"
Basketball *(August 8, 1930–February 11, 2015)*

Jerry Tarkanian is a Naismith Memorial Hall of Fame-inducted former NCAA and NBA basketball coach. He coached NCAA basketball for 31 years at three different schools. He led the UNLV Runnin' Rebels to the NCAA Championship in 1990. He also had a brief stint as the head coach for the San Antonio Spurs in 1992, but returned to NCAA coaching at UNLV shortly after the beginning of the season.

JEFF SAMARDZIJA, a.k.a. "The Shark"
Baseball *(born January 23, 1985)*

Jeff Samardzija is a professional Major League Baseball player for the San Francisco Giants. He played college football and baseball for Notre Dame and was named an All-American wide receiver. Other teams he has played for in the MLB include the Chicago Cubs, Chicago White Sox, and Oakland Athletics. Samardzija has previously stated that he got his nickname from his college pitching days because his fellow teammates said his smile looked like Bruce, the shark from the Disney film *Finding Nemo*.

GREG NORMAN, a.k.a. "The Great White Shark"
Golf *(born February, 10, 1955)*

Probably the most well-known shark athlete on this list, Greg Norman played professional golf from 1976 until his last professional contest in 2009 and has racked up many accolades over the course of his illustrious golfing career. He has won 91 international tournaments, including 20 PGA tournaments and 2 PGA championships, and was inducted into the World Golf Hall of Fame in 2001. He now mostly participates in his philanthropic endeavors and a huge entrepreneurial empire that includes golf course design services, wines, a clothing line, and restaurants.

HUMBERTO BRENES, a.k.a. "The Shark"
Poker *(born May 8, 1951)*

Humberto Brenes is a professional poker player from Costa Rica. By 2013, he had accumulated over $6,000,000 in tournament winnings. He currently plays for Team PokerStars. He got his nickname from a small toy shark that he uses as a card protector and good luck charm when playing poker.

KENNETH GANT, a.k.a. "The Shark"
American Football *(born April 18, 1967)*

Kenneth Gant is a former professional NFL football player who played for the Dallas Cowboys and the Tampa Bay Buccaneers. He helped the Cowboys defeat the Buffalo Bills twice in Super Bowls XXVII and XXVIII to win two NFL Championships. His celebratory dance was affectionately known as the "Shark Dance." (And it's actually quite complex!)

MARK SHRADER, a.k.a. "The Shark"
Professional Wrestling *(born September 9, 1967)*

Mark Shrader is a former professional wrestler who was popular in the East Coast and Mid-Atlantic "indies circuit" during his wrestling career between 1993 and 2003. The majority of his career was in the lesser known wrestling leagues in the United States, but he briefly appeared as a preliminary wrestler in the World Wrestling Federation. Two of his signature moves are also shark related, being called the "Shark Attack" and "Shark Frenzy."

MARK SELBY, a.k.a. "Mark the Shark"
Snooker and Pool *(born June 19, 1983)*

Mark Selby is a professional pool and snooker player from the United Kingdom. In 2016, he won the World Snooker Championship for the third year in a row. He has won many other titles in his illustrious professional career that began at the young age of 15. His other professional nickname is the "Jester from Leicester," referring to his hometown in the UK.

REAL, PROP, OR CG?

The debut of Jaws in 1975 really paved the way for a whole genre of shark horror and disaster flicks. But in the myriad of shark-threat movies, only a few got to hit the theaters (most killer shark movies are direct-to-video or guilty pleasure TV movies). Can you tell if the sharks in these theatrical releases were filmed using a real shark, a prop shark, or computer-generated shark? Circle every correct answer—some movies use multiple effects!

1. *Dark Tide* (2012)
Starring Halle Berry and Olivier Martinez

A dive instructor returns to the water after a near-fatal encounter with a great white.

REAL   PROP   CG

2. *Deep Blue Sea* (1999)

> Starring Thomas Jane, Samuel L. Jackson, and LL Cool J

A group of scientists working on a cure for Alzheimer's disease experiment on mako shark brains. Guess what? The sharks got smarter, and they're not happy.

REAL   PROP   CG

3. *Jaws* (1975)

> Starring Roy Scheider, Robert Shaw, and Richard Dreyfuss

A fisherman, a scientist, and a policeman team up to stop a great white shark from terrorizing the island town of Amity.

REAL   PROP   CG

4. *Open Water* (2003)

Starring Blanchard Ryan and Daniel Travis

A harrowing survival flick that's loosely based on a true story about a couple who gets accidentally stranded during a scuba diving trip and must fend for themselves by treading water in shark-infested waters in the Caribbean.

REAL   PROP   CG

5. *The Shallows* (2016)

Starring Blake Lively

Similar to *Open Water*, a surfer finds herself in a battle for survival against a great white shark.

REAL   PROP   CG

ANSWER:

DARK TIDE: Real + CG. In the movie, Halle Berry played a diving expert dubbed "The Shark Whisperer," but in real life, she actually did get to touch one of the live great whites while filming in South Africa, citing it as an extremely unique experience.

DEEP BLUE SEA: Real + Prop + CG. This cult favorite's got the hat trick of using all three. The trio of mutated mako sharks was mostly a combination of computer graphics and animatronic props. And the massive shark robot that ate Samuel L. Jackson's character currently resides in the St. George Spirits distillery in Alameda, CA, with a fantastic view of the San Francisco bay.

JAWS: Real + Prop. Nicknamed "Flaws" during filming, Jaws had a ton of problems, from disgruntled crew members and going way over budget to problematic actors and malfunctioning pneumatic shark props. The latter proved to be saviors of the film, as director Steven Spielberg describes them. The wonky and finicky animatronic sharks forced the team to work around and employ more minimalistic film effects, such as shooting only the dorsal fin above water and hinting at the shark more than showing it. Live sharks were used for the cage scene with Richard Dreyfuss.

OPEN WATER: Real. Yup, the sharks (and probably the actors' fear) in this film were real, and praised by critics. Chris Kentis and Laura Lau, the husband-and-wife team who wrote, directed, and filmed the movie are both divers and insisted on using live sharks in natural waters versus in a studio tank. How did they achieve this? Shark experts handled dozens of grey reef sharks that are not prone to attack, and the casted actors were certified divers and wore chainmail underneath their wetsuits, you know, *just in case.*

THE SHALLOWS: CG. Director Jaume Collet-Serra noted that only 10 percent of the movie was shot on location, and the rest was filmed in a tank with a green screen. Blake Lively's onscreen nemesis was entirely computer generated but her onscreen costar, Steven Seagull, was a real seagull that had some real acting chops. As Collet-Serra describes it, "He was kind of like the Marlon Brando of seagulls."

CRYPTOQUOTE PART 4

In this last cryptogram, we have a shark-inspired quote about reading from the irreplaceable Douglas Adams. Each letter stands for another. Try to look for certain letter patterns: single letters by themselves are probably an A, contractions usually are -'RE, -'NT, or -'VE, and of course, the word "SHARK" may appear a few times. Unused letters are noted as well.

PUZZLE LETTER = ANSWER LETTER

A =

B =

C = not used

D =

E =

F = not used

G =

H = not used

I =

J =

K =

L = not used

M =

N =

O =

P =

Q = not used

R =

S =

T =

U =

V =

W =

X =

Y =

Z =

"SGGZT OPD TBOPZT...
"_____ ___ _____...
SDWONTD TBOPZT BOMD
_____ _____ ____
SDDY OPGNYE RGP O MDPA
____ _____ ___ _ ____
JGYK IXVD. IBDPD UDPD
____ ____. _____ ____
TBOPZT SDRGPD IBDPD UDPD
_____ _____ _____ ____
EXYGTONPT, OYE IBD PDOTGY
_____, ___ ___ _____
TBOPZT OPD TIXJJ XY IBD
_____ ___ _____ __ ___
GWDOY XT IBOI YGIBXYK XT
_____ __ ____ _____ __
SDIIDP OI SDXYK O TBOPZ
_____ __ _____ _ _____
IBOY O TBOPZ."
____ _ _____."
"

—Douglas Adams, author of
The Hitchhiker's Guide to the Galaxy

ANSWERS:

A = Y	J = L	S = B
B = H	K = G	T = S
C = not used	L = not used	U = W
D = E	M = V	V = M
E = D	N = U	W = C
F = not used	O = A	X = I
G = O	P = R	Y = N
H = not used	Q = not used	Z = K
I = T	R = F	

"BOOKS ARE SHARKS...
BECAUSE SHARKS HAVE
BEEN AROUND FOR A VERY
LONG TIME. THERE WERE
SHARKS BEFORE THERE
WERE DINOSAURS, AND THE
REASON SHARKS ARE STILL IN
THE OCEAN IS THAT NOTHING
IS BETTER AT BEING A SHARK
THAN A SHARK."

—Douglas Adams, author of
The Hitchhiker's Guide to the Galaxy

BIT OF SPORT FISHIN'

Different kinds of sharks can be found in all of the oceans in the world, but did you know you can find them on the sidelines of many professional sports games as well? Below is a list of professional sports teams across the world that have decided to have a shark as their mascot. Check out their jawsome "spokesanimals," and then try to find their names in a word search puzzle!

San Jose Sharks—
S.J. Sharkie

Perhaps the most well-known shark mascot, S.J. Sharkie has been with the team since its inception in 1992. He even won the coveted title of "Most Awesome Mascot" by the Cartoon Network!

Nova Southeastern Sharks—
Razor

Nova Southeastern University is an NCAA Division I team in the Sunshine State Conference. Their mascot Razor, a mako shark, was voted as the new mascot in

2005, joining the brethren of many fishy Floridian team mascots.

Worcester Sharks—
FINZ

The Sharks of Worcester, Massachusetts, are the American Hockey League affiliation team for the San Jose Sharks. The beloved FINZ (yes, his name is in all-caps) retired in 2015 when the team moved to San Jose and was rebranded as the San Jose Barracudas.

Cronulla-Sutherland Sharks—
MC Hammerhead and **Reefy**

The Cronulla-Sutherland Sharks of the National Rugby League in Australia have not only one, but two shark mascots! MC Hammerhead, of course, is a hammerhead, and Reefy is a great white shark.

JUPITER Hammerheads—
Hamilton R. Head

The Jupiter Hammerheads are a minor league baseball team in the Florida State League and are the Class A affiliate of the Miami Marlins. Their mascot, Hamilton R. Head, is a hammerhead shark who actually gets his name from former Secretary of the US Department of the Treasury, hero, and scholar, Alexander Hamilton.

Clearwater Threshers—
Phinley

The Clearwater Threshers are another shark-themed team in the Florida State League and are the Class A affiliate for the Philadelphia Phillies. Their mascot is Phinley, carefully and deliberately spelled with a "Ph" instead of an "F" to pay homage to the Phillies' mascot, the Philly Phanatic.

Jacksonville Sharks—
Chum

The Jacksonville Sharks are a former Arena Football League and current National Arena League football team. Their mascot Chum is the only mascot on this list who is actually not a shark–he's human! Legend has it that Chum has a gift for talking to and befriending sharks, and was even kicked out of his old fishing town where he grew up for secretly throwing all the bait into the water so that the local sharks wouldn't get caught.

East Fremantle Sharks—
Shredder

The mascot of the East Fremantle Sharks of the West Australian Football League is named Shredder. The East Fremantle Sharks have both a men's and a women's team. Not only does Shredder come out to the games and local events to support the team, he's also known for penning news articles for the squads. No reports yet on how Shredder holds a pen or work a keyboard.

Sale Sharks—
Sharky and **Finlay**

The Sale Sharks are an English rugby club based in Barton-upon-Irwell, Salford, England, and play in the English Premiership rugby union. Sharky and Finlay are twin brothers, separated at birth and reunited on the rugby field! Good thing adelphophagy didn't occur between the two.

University of South Carolina Beaufort Sand Sharks—
Finnegan

The name Finnegan handily won a contest to become the University of South Carolina Beaufort's new mascot, beating out "Chomp," "Thrasher," and "Sandy," with 57 percent of the votes.

```
D V Q D D A J P S F E B Q W F I
T A P V A F C H A M K F W N Y F
T Z E N E E P I Z A Q A W G I K
J Z N H H V O N G L F L P N M Y
S R D W R T S L V R A X L E I A
O R T O E N J E T T L A I G J H
T I O I M Z O Y S K Y K R A H S
M W S Z M G Y T R H R F I N Z X
D Z Q C A O Y E L A R I L X S U
F J F T H R D J H I I E R Y N L
P N W M C G U S F J M L D P Y Y
Z O U R M V J A G H F A Q D F T
A H J L R S P E S R A O H Q E A
C D H R S A F I N N E G A N E R
B L K W T I W Q V L B W T U R N
Y L M M F K K P U F L I I X B Q
```

KEY:

CHUM

FINLAY

FINNEGAN

FINZ

HAMILTONRHEAD

MCHAMMERHEAD

PHINLEY

RAZOR

REEFY

SHARKY

SHREDDER

SJSHARKIE

ANSWER:

```
D V Q D D A J P S F E B Q W F I
T A P V A F C H A M K F W N Y F
T Z E N E P I Z A Q A W G I K
J Z N H V O N G L F L P N M Y
S R D W R T S L V R A X L E I A
O R T O E N J E T T L A I G J H
T I O I M Z O Y S K Y K R A H S
M W S Z M G Y T R H R F I N Z X
D Z Q C A O Y E L A R I L X S U
F J F T H R D J H I I E R Y N L
P N W M C G U S F J M L D P Y Y
Z O U R M V J A G H F A Q D F T
A H J L R S P E S R A O H Q E A
C D H R S A F I N N E G A N E R
B L K W T I W Q V L B W T U R N
Y L M M F K K P U F L I I X B Q
```

LE FIN

Here's hoping that you enjoyed our wondrous, finformative journey. Before we swim into the sunset with our Ray-Bans on and cocktails in hand, it's time to get schooled one last time. So mako way for one last challenge, and see how much you've learned about sharks.

CLUES:

ACROSS

2. Technical term for the shark's nose

5. A group of sharks (and what you do when you see one)

9. Rubbery shark skeleton material

10. Hagfish boon

11. Largest extinct shark

12. Cretoxyrhina's sharp nickname

14. Golf shark Greg

16. Type of shark that supposedly helps moms and newborns

17. Oceanic white tip's BFF

20. Bubblegum-pink shark named after a folklore monster

21. Bullshark doppelganger

22. Shark meat from down under

24. Proper name for fish tail

25. Iconic *Jaws* part peeking through water

26. Shark type of 25

DOWN

1. Molecular compound that helps sharks survive in salt water

3. What baby sand sharks eat in the womb

4. Fish whiskers

6. Oily organ

7. Fish food hodgepodge

8. Can move between freshwater and salt water

10. Common shark fin dish

13. Where SAP Center, aka "The Shark Tank," is

15. He was the one who jumped the shark

16. Fastest shark there is

17. Shark youngling

18. State with heavy shark activity

19. Halle Berry flick

23. Peter Benchley novel

ANSWER:

ACROSS

2. ROSTRUM

5. SHIVER

9. CARTILAGE

10. SLIME

11. MEGALODON

12. GINSU

14. NORMAN

16. MILK

17. PILOT

20. GOBLIN SHARK

21. PIGEYE

22. FLAKE

24. CAUDAL

25. DORSAL

26. WHITE

DOWN

1. UREA

3. SIBLINGS

4. BARBEL

6. LIVER

7. CHUM

8. DIADROMOUS

10. SOUP

13. SAN JOSE

15. FONZIE

16. MAKO

17. PUP

18. FLORIDA

19. DARK TIDE

23. JAWS

ARTWORK CREDITS

Artwork from shutterstock.com

© maritime m: seaweed in folios

© AKorolchuk: page 4

© ALBRAGA: pages 27, 34-35, 99, 157, 241-42

© chekart: answer fins and page 1

© Cozynook: pages 12-13, 68, 72, 79-80, 88, 103, 119, 128, 165, 168

© evgo1977: pages 2, 46, 70, 82, 87, 136, 138, 160, 192, 202, 204, 238

© Farhad Bek: pages 16-17, 32, 126, 172

© Hein Nouwens: page 8

© IADA: pages 3, 71, 139, 193

© KUCO: pages iv-v, 6-7, 10, 14-15, 20, 36-43, 50-51, 56, 59, 62, 64-66, 73-74, 77-78, 84-85, 92-94, 106, 110, 118, 124, 142-43, 146, 149-50, 152-54, 158, 163-64, 171, 179, 194-97, 200, 208, 214, 248

© lupulluss: pages 18-19, 184-87

© matyas: pages 5, 28, 30, 76, 96, 166, 182, 213, 218

© Mayboroda: page 210

© pinare: pages 108, 111, 130-33, 232, 233

© stasia_ch: page 229

© tristan tan: pages 22, 24-25, 81, 90-91, 100-101, 140-41, 175, 216

© tugce ersoy: pages 44, 104-105, 115, 120, 122, 206-207

© ziiinvn: page 144

ACKNOWLEDGMENTS

I would like to thank:

Dear to my heart and dear to my brain, my pub quiz and *Good Job, Brain!* crew Colin, Dana, and Chris, who have endured way too many of my very excited and graphically detailed tellings of how different marine animals mate.

Cameron, who is my pilot fish.

Friends, family, and you, dear reader, whose support pushes me to always learn more about and experience more of our wacky little planet.

Stay curious!

ABOUT THE AUTHOR

Karen Chu is a trivia enthusiast and avid pub quiz player. She brews mead, runs marathons in costume, and is way into vexillology. She hosts and produces the award-winning trivia podcast *Good Job, Brain!* and enjoys learning about the bizarre ways animals reproduce, with the angler fish being on the top of that list.